IMAGES
of England

The Duke of Cornwall's Light Infantry

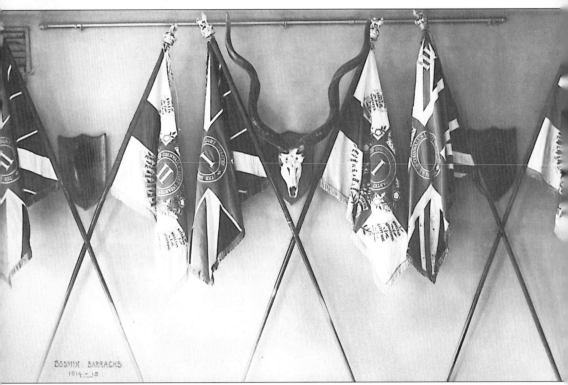

BODMIN BARRACKS
1914 - 15

The Colours of the 1st, 2nd, and 3rd Battalions of the Duke of Cornwall's Light Infantry lodged at the Regimental Depot during the First World War. To understand this book one must understand what the Regiment means to a British infantry soldier. In other armies of the world a regiment is an operational formation to which officers and soldiers are attached for routine tours of duty. To the British infantryman, his Regiment is his family. He becomes a member of this family on the day he joins, and usually remains with it throughout his entire service. The cap badge worn with such pride by all ranks from the Colonel to the newly joined recruit as a symbol of this close knit society. The Regiment provides the security and close comradeship of a strong family; in return it demands absolute and total loyalty. In battle the infantryman is usually exhausted, filthy, hungry and frightened. Few men have the resources to stand up to these conditions on their own. Pride of Regiment gives men that inner strength to rise above themselves and make any sacrifice rather than let their comrades down.

IMAGES
of England

THE DUKE OF CORNWALL'S LIGHT INFANTRY

Compiled by
Hugo White

TEMPUS

First published 2000
Copyright © Hugo White, 2000

Tempus Publishing Limited
The Mill, Brimscombe Port,
Stroud, Gloucestershire, GL5 2QG

ISBN 0 7524 1893 9

Typesetting and origination by
Tempus Publishing Limited
Printed in Great Britain by
Midway Clark Printing, Wiltshire

Cover illustration: In 1899 Lady Inglis laid the foundation stone of the Memorial to the officers and men of the 32nd Light Infantry who were killed or died during the siege of Lucknow in 1857. Lady Inglis was the widow of Major-General Sir John Inglis, late of the 32nd, who had commanded the Lucknow Garrison during the siege. She had herself been present throughout, together with her son. This photograph shows Lady Inglis on the occasion of the foundation stone ceremony. Left to right, back row: Sjt-Maj. Peel, Lt Carter (later to win the Victoria Cross), Lt Williams-Freeman, Lt Hearsey (Quartermaster). Front row: Lt-Col. Turnbull (Commanding Officer), Mrs Ashton (daughter of Lady Inglis), Lady Inglis, Mrs Turnbull, Lt Bliss (Adjutant).

Contents

Acknowledgements

I would like to thank Maj. Richard Vyvyan-Robinson MBE and the Trustees of the Duke of Cornwall's Light Infantry Museum for the use of the majority of the photographs reproduced in this book. My thanks are also due to the Imperial War Museum for their permission to reproduce the pictures on pp. 109 and 110 and the Cornwall County Records Office for their permission to reproduce the picture on p. 20.

The book could certainly not have been completed without the computer skills of Mrs Debbie Fisher, the typist in the Light Infantry Office (Cornwall). I am also indebted to Mr Joe Kendall, an ex bugler of the Regiment, Mr Alton Vincent, the DCLI Museum attendant, and Mrs Lauraine Sadleir, the administration assistant in the Light Infantry Office for spending many hours tracking down and sorting mountains of photographs.

WHW
March 2000

Introduction

Like every other county regiment, the Duke of Cornwall's Light Infantry came into existence in 1881 as a result of the sweeping reforms which had been initiated by Lord Cardwell. However, the two former constituent parts – the 32nd and the 46th Regiments – both date back to the eighteenth century.

Britain's involvement in the War of the Spanish Succession necessitated a considerable expansion of her armed forces. Thus it was that, on 1 June 1702, Queen Anne signed a warrant authorizing Colonel Edward Fox to raise a regiment of marines. This regiment, which was later to become the 32nd Foot, and later still the 1st Battalion Duke of Cornwall's Light Infantry, was largely recruited from Sussex. The following year it saw service under the ill-fated Admiral Sir Cloudesley Shovel, taking an active part in the capture of a Spanish treasure fleet in Vigo Bay. Over £1,000,000 worth of gold and silver bullion fell into British hands (equivalent to approximately £70,000,000 today). Every man who took part received a silver medal – the first time that the rank and file had ever been granted such an award. In 1704, what had been intended merely as a hit and run raid against the Spanish dockyard in Gibraltar ended up as the capture of that formidable fortress. Fox's Marines suffered very few casualties – indeed the battle was short and almost bloodless – but in the ensuing months and years the Rock was to endure a succession of the most terrible sieges.

In 1715 the Regiment became the 32nd Foot, a proud numeral that it was to bear for the next 166 years. It played a continuous part in every phase of the Peninsula Campaign from 1808 till 1814, and once again at the final victory of Waterloo in 1815. Routine soldiering in Ireland and Canada led up to its critical participation in a war which threatened the very existence of the British Empire – the Indian Mutiny of 1857. The 32nd Foot occupied the Residency compound, a position of vital tactical importance. For one hundred and fifty seven days, the garrison endured a siege by a vastly superior force. In recognition of its gallantry, Queen Victoria ordered that the Regiment should be honoured with the designation of 'Light Infantry'.

To turn to the other constituent part of the Duke of Cornwall's Light Infantry, the 46th Foot. The threat of insurrection in Scotland in the 1740s required additional land forces. On 13 January 1741, King George II issued a warrant to Colonel John Price authorizing him to raise a regiment of foot at Newcastle-on-Tyne. This regiment, originally numbered the 57th, immediately took part in what would now be termed 'Internal Security Operations', which were to culminate in the full blown rebellion of 1745. During the War of American Independence the Regiment, now numbered the 46th, was involved in a brilliant night attack against a rebel force at Paoli in 1777. The commander, General Grey, aware that an accidental discharge would compromise the whole operation, ordered that every man should remove the flint from his musket lock. The attack was therefore made with the bayonet, at least two hundred Americans being killed. Incensed by this act of 'brutal barbarity' the Americans let it be known that henceforth no quarter would be given to British prisoners. Those who took part in the attack – proud of their achievement – proclaimed that they alone were responsible and, so that they could be immediately recognised by their foes, would dye their cap feathers red. This red headdress embellishment became a feature of the 46th (and later the Duke of Cornwall's Light Infantry) from that time. Indeed the present Regiment – the Light Infantry – continues the tradition, wearing a red backing to the cap badge.

In 1881 the 32nd (Cornwall) Light Infantry and the 46th (South Devonshire) Regiment of Foot (county titles had been added in 1782) amalgamated to form the 1st and 2nd Battalions Duke of Cornwall's Light Infantry. The new Regiment was almost immediately involved in the Egyptian War of 1882, the Nile Expedition of 1884-85 and the South African War of 1899-1902. In the First World War it raised a total of fourteen battalions, eight of which saw action in France, Belgium, Italy, Salonika, Aden and Palestine, and one of which served in India. In the Second World War it raised six battalions, three of which saw action in France, Holland, Belgium, Germany, North Africa, Italy and Greece and one of which, although not seeing action, had the unglamorous but vital job of operating as pioneers in North Africa. In the last days of its history as the Duke of Cornwall's Light Infantry, the Regiment saw active service in Palestine, Cyprus and Somaliland beside carrying out garrison duties in the West Indies and long periods as part of the British Army of the Rhine.

With the British withdrawal from Empire, it was inevitable that her army should be radically reduced. Thus it was that a long series of amalgamations and disbandments was put in train during the 1950s, and that on 6 October 1959 the Duke of Cornwall's Light Infantry amalgamated with the Somerset Light Infantry (Prince Albert's) to form a new Regiment – the Somerset and Cornwall Light Infantry.

One
The 32nd and 46th Regiments of Foot 1702-1881

Up to 1881 most infantry regiments normally consisted of a single battalion. When serving in the United Kingdom they could replace wastage by a continuous programme of recruiting; however, when abroad, regiments had no satisfactory system of replacement so that their numbers fell until they inevitably reached a point at which they were not longer fit for service. They then had to be brought back home to conduct a major recruiting drive. In 1782, regiments were allotted county titles in an effort to rationalize the recruiting areas, thus the 32nd became the 32nd (Cornwall) Regiment and the 46th became the 46th (South Devonshire) Regiment. This, however, failed to address the key problem of how to maintain overseas regiments up to establishment.

This was also a period in which the power, wealth and influence of Great Britain was enormously expanded. The American Colonies were lost in 1781, but vast tracts of the World, principally in the sub-continent of India, fell under British rule. In this great power struggle the army played a major part, soldiering in virtually every corner of the Globe. Medical knowledge was still primitive, far more men dying of disease than at the hands of the enemy.

A copy of the Royal Warrant authorizing the raising of six Regiments of Marines and six additional Regiments of Foot dated 1 June 1702. The original was signed by Queen Anne. Fox's Marines (later the 32nd Foot) was one of those authorised in this warrant.

A Private of Fox's Marines, 1707.

A soldier of the Light Company, 46th Foot, in the American War of Independence, 1777.

10

The 3pdr infantry gun used by the 46th Foot in their heroic defence of a defile just inland from Rosseau on the island of Dominica on 22 February 1805. A Serjeant and seven men of the 46th held their ground and practically annihilated a French company at least ten times their own strength. These 3pdr guns, issued on a scale of two per battalion, must represent the very first use of infantry close support weapons. Although generally manhandled using 'man-harness', they could also be drawn by horses. Generally considered to be more trouble than they were worth, their use was discontinued around 1807. However, on this particular occasion the 3pdr undoubtedly justified its existence.

The death of Sir Thomas Picton at Waterloo, 18 June 1815. Two Grenadiers of the 32nd Foot are seen coming to their General's aid. Although this illustration was painted by Ensign John Morris of the 32nd, who was present, it is not strictly accurate. Sir Thomas Picton seldom wore uniform on active service, and at Waterloo was wearing a civilian frock coat and broad brimmed top hat.

11

The King's Colour of the 32nd Foot was briefly seized by a French officer at Waterloo on 18 June 1815. His triumph however was short-lived; he was killed almost instantly by Ensign Birtwhistle, who had been carrying the Colour, and by the escort, Sjt Switzer.

A group of 46th Foot Officers in the Crimea, 1855. Left to right: Ensign Thomas Forde, Col. Robert Garrett, Capt. Algernon Garrett, Lt-Col. Alexander Maxwell. The partly underground hut seen in the background is typical of the living accommodation behind the lines which was constructed after the first winter. Note how full dress has been abandoned in favour of more serviceable clothing. Only the newly joined Ensign continues to wear his scarlet undress shelljacket. The name of the officer on the extreme right is not known.

A group of officers, including several from the 46th, probably taken at the end of the Crimean War. Many of the officers wear the loose, double-breasted scarlet tunic introduced in 1855 and superseded in 1857. This photograph demonstrates two features of military life that still apply today: first, a love of dogs; secondly, the impossibility of ever gathering a group of officers together wearing the same order of dress!

An early photograph of a soldier of the Duke of Cornwall's Rangers (Rifles) Militia. The Militia was a conscript force under the control of the Lord Lieutenant whose soldiers were recruited by selected ballot. Men could opt out of their commitment on payment of a 'fine' of £10, providing they could find a willing replacement. This man is armed with the 1853 short pattern Enfield rifle with its heavy and unwieldy Yatagan sword bayonet.

Part of the Residency Building which formed the hub of the defensive position during the siege. The Defence of Lucknow in 1857 by a garrison largely consisting of the 32nd (Cornwall) Regiment of Foot is deemed to have been the finest chapter in the Regiment's long history. The anniversary of the final relief is still celebrated whenever old members of the Duke of Cornwall's can come together.

Up to 1857, the security of the British Raj in India was maintained, not principally by the British Army, but by a very large force of native troops under the control of a powerful trading consortium known as the East India Company. By the middle of the nineteenth century Indian nationalizm was emerging as a vocal force, and during the latter part of 1856 it was known that the Sepoys (Indian soldiers) were being subjected to strong subversive pressure.

In February 1857 the first mutinies broke out in Barrackpore and Berhampore. Quickly insurrection spread to cover most native troops in the Province of Oudh. In May, the great military fortress of Delhi fell to the rebels giving them access to vast quantities of weapons and ammunition. Under their leader, Nana Sahib, the triumphant force of mutineers started to move south down the Ganges towards the Imperial Capital of Calcutta. There was little to hinder their progress except the small garrison at Lucknow, commanded by Sir Henry Lawrence.

On 27 June the garrison at Cawnpore (30 miles from Lucknow) was massacred. Three days later the Lucknow garrison made a pre-emptive strike against the rebels at Chinhat. It was a disaster. Casualties, which included the Commanding Officer of the 32nd, were heavy and the British withdrew into the perimeter of the Residency which they proceeded to turn into a strong defensive position. By the evening of 30 June the garrison was surronded by a vastly superior rebel army.

On 4 July General Sir Henry Lawrence was killed. Lt-Col. John Inglis of the 32nd took over command. Exhausted, sick and increasingly short of food, water and ammunition the gallant defenders held their ground against countless assaults. Indeed, the battle was frequently taken into enemy territory by courageous groups who sallied out to destroy rebel guns.

On 25 September a brigade under General Sir Henry Havelock fought its way into Lucknow, supplying a much needed reinforcement to the ragged and dwindling garrison. However, it was not until 17 November that Lucknow was finally relieved by the main British Force under General Sir Colin Campbell.

The 32nd can claim to have played a vital part in the frustration of Nana Sahib's campaign to capture Calcutta. Had he succeeded, the whole future of a British presence in India would have been in grave doubt. This is one of the few instances in which the determination of a single battalion changed the course of history. For their gallantry at Lucknow, Queen Victoria commanded that the 32nd Foot should be designated a Regiment of Light Infantry.

Ensign William Studdy, 32nd Foot, probably photographed on his arrival with the Regiment in India in 1856. In spite of the heat and dirt, short hair was not considered acceptable by either officers or men. Studdy's service with the 32nd was tragically short, as he died of wounds received at Lucknow on 9 August 1857. The short scarlet shell jacket was the standard uniform in India at that time, however during the Mutiny dress became very much more relaxed. During the hot weather jackets were discarded and loose cotton shirts were worn outside cotton trousers. Both shirts and trousers were dyed with tea – an early form of camouflage.

Cpl William Oxenham, 32nd Foot, who was awarded the Victoria Cross for distinguished gallantry on 30 June 1857 at Lucknow, for rescuing Mr Capper of the Bengal Civil Service while exposed to heavy and close fire. William Oxenham came from Tiverton in Devon.

Lt Henry Gore-Browne, 32nd Foot, who was awarded the Victoria Cross for conspicuous bravery during the Siege of Lucknow. This award was given, in particular, for his gallantry in leading a sortie on 24 August 1857, at great personal risk, for the purpose of spiking two heavy guns. Both guns were rendered unusable and around a hundred enemy were killed. Henry Gore-Browne came from Roscommon in Ireland.

Lt Samuel Hill-Lawrence, 32nd Foot, who was awarded the Victoria Cross for distinguished bravery in leading a sortie at Lucknow on 7 July 1857. He was also decorated for leading a sortie on 26 September 1857 in which two 9pdr guns were destroyed. Samuel Hill-Lawrence came from Cork in Ireland. He later purchased a transfer to the 11th Hussars. This photograph shows him in the uniform of the latter Regiment.

The ruins of the Dikusha Palace just east of Lucknow. This was an important rebel stronghold which lay in the path of Sir Colin Campbells relieving force. It was captured on 14 November 1857 after a savage battle. Sir Henry Havelock, the leader of the first relieving force, died of enteric fever in this building a few days after the siege had been raised.

The fort at Cawnpore under the command of Gen. Wheeler, held an important tactical position on the Ganges. As the Indian Mutiny developed, it became a safe haven for Europeans and, by June 1857, contained some 500 men, women and children. The principal military element of the garrison consisted of a company of the 32nd under Capt. Moore. In spite of having plenty of time to plan his defence, Gen. Wheeler failed to lay in supplies and made little preparation to withstand a siege. After a month, in which the garrison experienced the most appalling privations of heat, thirst and hunger, it surrendered on 26 June. Having promised the garrison safe passage down the Ganges, the rebel leader, Nana Sahib, reneged on his word and ordered every European – man, woman and child – to be butchered. Of the entire garrison, only four made their escape.

The Baillie Guard Gate leading into the Residency compound at Lucknow. The gate, which was heavily reinforced on the inside with earth and stones, was the focus of almost continuous rebel assaults throughout the siege.

The ruins of the Residency with the monument to the dead of the 32nd Foot in the foreground. In memory of the gallant defence, in 1857, the Union Flag seen flying from the tower was the only one in the British Empire never to be lowered at sunset.

Pte William Dicker, who served with the 46th Foot during the Crimean War, photographed wearing the new pattern tunic which supplanted the original short lived double breasted version in 1857.

Bugler George Bogue, 32nd Light Infantry, was born in Newcastle-upon-Tyne and originally enlisted in the North Durham Militia. He transferred to the 32nd as a bugler in 1859 and served for ten years with the Colours in Ireland, Gibraltar and Mauritius. After leaving the Army he was employed as Superintendent of Labour at Kendal Workhouse.

The 6th Cornwall Rifle Volunteers relaxing after drill at Launceston Castle in May 1861. The uniform, reminiscent of French troops of the period, is grey with black or dark blue sleeve knots. The rifles 'piled' at the back of the group are 1853 pattern Enfields.

Lt John Low was commissioned into the 46th Foot in 1862. This photograph was taken when the Regiment was stationed on the Isle of Wight in 1868. Why he is wearing Canadian winter clothing standing in front of a painted snow scene remains a mystery. As far as can be ascertained he never served in North Canada, nor was the Regiment warned for that station.

The Serjeants of the 46th Foot at Aldershot in 1871.

A group of officers of the 46th Foot at The Curragh in Ireland in 1874. The informality of these early photographs contrasts with the rigid poses adopted in regimental groups fifty years later.

Officers of the 46th Foot at the Beggar's Bush Barracks, Dublin, in 1874. The heavily built, bewhiskered officer in the front row is Lt-Col. Charles Catty. He had led an exceptionally dangerous and exciting life during the Kaffir War, 1850-53, in which he raised, trained and commanded a highly unconventional irregular force of Europeans which came to be known as 'Catty's Rifles'. These men became experts in deep penetration patrolling and on many occasions provided invaluable information.

Officers of the 46th Foot probably at the Curragh, Ireland, in 1874. The braided blue patrol jacket shown here would have been the normal everyday wear in camp. The officer on the right with the white dog on his lap is the Adjutant, Lt Charles de la Poer Beresford.

The 46th Foot practising battle drills at the Curragh, Ireland, in 1875. Although these close order formations may look totally archaic today, one must remember that they were designed for fighting in theatres such as Zululand or Abyssinia in which small bodies of soldiers armed with single shot rifles had to stand up to attacks by vast hordes of poorly armed tribesmen. Tight formations protected by a hedge of bayonets often provided the best means of defence.

Maj.-Gen. William Lacy was commissioned into the 46th Foot in 1826. He spent most of his fifty-one years of service as 'Staff Captain of Pensioners' in the rank of captain, but was promoted to Honorary Major General on his retirement in 1877 when this photograph was taken.

Officers of the Royal Cornwall Rangers, Duke of Cornwall's Own Regiment of Militia, photographed on the steps of Shire House, Bodmin, in April 1879. This Regiment appears to have had a remarkable propensity for changing its title, no fewer than six of these changes occurring in the nineteenth century alone. Although the Militia had ceased to be under the direct control of the Lord-Lieutenant since 1871, it was still officered almost entirely by the county's landed gentry. This group shows two Onslows, an Eliot, three St Aubyns, two Trelawnys, two Vyvyans, a Bickford-Smith and a Hext. The officer wearing a cocked hat in the back row is the Regimental Medical Officer, Surgeon Major Thomas Quiller Couch, father of the famous Cornish author, Sir Arthur Quiller Couch.

Two
The Climax of Empire
1881-1914

The British Army has always been adamantly conservative when defending its traditions. It was therefore against the most bitter opposition from the military establishment that Lord Cardwell forced through his various Army Reform Acts which led to the radical reorganization of the infantry in 1881. Under this Act, the old, single battalion, numbered regiments were grouped in pairs to produce new county regiments, each containing two battalions. One of these battalions, kept at full establishment, would serve overseas while the other – 'the Home Battalion' – would look after recruiting and provide reinforcement drafts. In addition, a new depôt barracks was built for each new regiment within its recruiting area where recruits could be trained. Last but not least, the Act brought the somewhat haphazardly organized units of Volunteers and Militia firmly into the new regimental system.

The 32nd and 46th of Foot became the 1st and 2nd Battalions of the Duke of Cornwall's Light Infantry with a depôt in Bodmin. This period marked the very peak of Britain's immense power, when it was firmly believed that the sun could never set on her Empire.

Regimental Quartermaster Sjt Burns of the 2nd Volunteer Battalion is seen in 1881, just after the Volunteers became part of the Duke of Cornwall's Light Infantry. The numerous badges and the medal, somewhat reminiscent of a Boy Scout, appear to be rifle-shooting awards. Burns wears a strange hybrid uniform which combines the new DCLI scarlet tunic with the leather accoutrements of the former Rifle Volunteers.

A posed photograph showing the orders of dress worn by the 2nd Battalion in the field during the Egyptian Campaign of 1882. The Pioneer Serjeant, fourth from the right, sports a beard, which was traditional to his appointment. The tall figure, fourth from the left, with a drawn revolver is the Sjt-Maj. George Carr. Many contemporary accounts remark on how inappropriate scarlet serge was for wear in the heat of the Egyptian summer and how filthy and sweat stained it became.

Depôt transport on the barrack square at Bodmin 1882.

The entrance gate of the Depôt in 1882.

The landing party from HMS *Invincible* which played a prominent part in the Egyptian Campaign of 1882. This is an armoured train improvised by the ship's artificers mounting a 40pdr gun taken from the ship, and carrying a number of light field guns similar to those used at the Royal Tournament up to 1999. This train saw action to the left of the 2nd Battalion position at the Battle of Tel-el-Kebir on 13 September 1882.

A section of men from the 2nd Battalion at Pembroke Dock Barracks in 1889. Close order formations like this were still used in many operational theatres in which a soldier might be called upon to fight. The Martini-Henry rifle with its immensely long 21inch bayonet was however already obsolescent, being in process of replacement by the magazine Lee-Metford.

The 2nd Battalion Signallers at Pembroke Dock Barracks in 1889. This clearly shows the three principal systems of signalling at that time – flag, lamp and heliograph. The 5inch heliographs, shown here at the extreme left and right of the group, operated by reflecting sunlight down a narrow beam. Under good conditions, with sufficiently long lines of sight, ranges of about 70 miles could be achieved.

The Bugles of the 2nd Battalion at Pembroke Dock in 1890. Note the heavy and cumbersome short swords which drummers and buglers carried as part of their dress at that period. The senior NCO in the centre is Bugle Serjeant Holloway who had served throughout the Egyptian and Sudan campaigns. The officer in the centre is the Adjutant, Lt E.S. Burder. The Bugles were presumably capable of providing a small informal concert group, hence the presence of the two banjos, which were certainly not used on parade! The small boy in the front, holding a kitten, is the son of L/Cpl R. Jones, sitting next to the Adjutant.

Changing 2nd Battalion sentries on the Dublin Castle Guard in 1891. The British presence in Dublin Castle, the official residence of the Viceroy of Ireland, provided a focus for Republican hatred and was consequently heavily protected against Feinian attack.

The Signal Section 2nd Volunteer Battalion, possibly at Tregantle Fort, Cornwall, in about 1890.

A peaceful scene: the 2nd Battalion fox hounds being exercised near Dublin in 1891.

Serjeant Bugler R. Jones of the 2nd Battalion in Dublin in 1892. Sjt Jones and his young son also appear in the photograph on p. 29 when Jones was a Lance Corporal. The Serjeant Buglers of Light Infantry normally carried short staffs but one must remember that the 2nd Battalion had only been Light Infantry for eleven years and was still very proud of its 46th Foot traditions, hence the longer staffs.

The 2nd Battalion football team, Dublin, 1891. How would our footballers today take to the fashions of a century ago?

The 2nd Battalion marching to the Queen's Birthday parade in Dublin, June 1893. The Battalion is led by the Pioneers carrying their axes and shovels. Note the Pioneer Serjeant on the right of the front rank wearing a beard, traditional to this appointment.

Buglers of the 2nd Battalion, probably in Newry, Ireland, in 1894. The Lance Corporal on the left is wearing the badge of the Commanding Officer's bugler. The six young figures in the group are Bugle Boys. At this period boy soldiers were enlisted between the ages of fourteen and sixteen.

The 1st Battalion tug-of-war team at Chakatra in 1895. In spite of having very short hair, soldiers were able to sport elaborate styles by the liberal use of pomade. The gentleman in plain clothes, seated in the centre, is the Commanding Officer, Lt-Col. Charles Turnbull.

Although this is an obviously posed photograph, it shows how married British Army Officers transplanted their Edwardian lifestyle to India in the early years of the twentieth century.

Regimental Mess tables positively groaned under the weight of silver with which they were decorated for festive occasions. This is the 1st Battalion silver, much of which is still in current use. Although a few of the items are of some antiquity, most of the largest and most flamboyant pieces date from the last years of the nineteenth century when the price of silver reached an all time low.

A married officer and his wife with their servants probably at Lucknow in 1896. Native staffs of this size were certainly not considered abnormal by the standards of the time.

Lady Inglis, widow of Maj.-Gen. Sir John Inglis, lays the foundation stone of the 32nd Foot Lucknow Memorial in 1897. Sir John Inglis was an officer of the 32nd who took over command of the garrison at Lucknow when the Resident, Sir Henry Lawrence, was killed on 2 July 1857. He conducted a masterly defence of the Residency compound against overwhelming odds from that date until the final relief on 17 November.

The 1st Battalion saw active service with the 3rd Brigade during the Tirah Campaign of 1897-98 – a punitive expedition against the tribesmen on the Peshawar-Kohat border who had been mounting raids against their neighbours. This photograph shows a tented camp in the Bara Valley towards the end of the campaign. All frontier tribesmen were adept at exploiting the slightest tactical error of their opponents. In particular, they would infiltrate dominating positions from which they could snipe at their enemies. Consequently every peak had to be securely held by a picquet – an operation which, given the nature of the terrain, required a high degree of physical fitness.

Officers at Ranikhet in 1897. Although this photograph shows officers who were not all from the Duke of Cornwall's Light Infantry, it clearly illustrates the army's age-old love of dogs.

Officers of the 1st Battalion in the Bara Valley camp. As was normal on active service, a certain latitude of dress seems to have been tolerated. The sticks and staves carried by many of those in the group would have been very necessary in negotiating this steep, rocky country. The officer sitting second from the left is from the Cameronian Rifles and was presumably attached to the Battalion.

The Serjeants of the 1st Battalion at Rawal Pindi in 1897. Note the leather Slade-Wallis equipment which, although blancoed white in peacetime, was invariably left in its natural matt colour when on active service. The Pioneer Serjeant, fourth from the left in the second row down, wears a beard traditional to his appointment.

A native field bakery in the 3rd Brigade camp in the Bara Valley.

A 1st Battalion picquet on a peak overlooking the Bara Valley. The scale of this rugged terrain can be judged from the size of the figures standing on a rock just to the left of the summit.

The Cycle Club at Allahabad, in 1897, which used to meet on Thursday mornings. Several of the gentlemen are officers of the 1st Battalion which was then stationed there. No European would have dreamt of venturing out into the sun without wearing suitable head protection. This photograph demonstrates the many varied styles of solar topee that were available. Capt. Ernest Burder, commanding 'G' Company, stands fourth from the right.

A remarkable feat of railway engineering. The narrow gauge line running up to Darjeeling, climbing from the plains to nearly 8,000 feet. The 1st Battalion used this railway *en route* to Lebong in 1898.

Another view of Darjeeling railway. By a process of going forwards and backwards over a series of zigzags, trains could be made to climb near precipitous slopes.

A view taken from a 1st Battalion picquet in the Khyber Pass near Ali Musjid Fort in 1898.

The Temperance Lodge of the 1st Battalion Band at Rawal Pindi in 1898. The problems associated with heavy drinking afflicted all levels of society in the nineteenth century, and none more so than the army in India, where cheap and potentially lethal native liquor was readily available. Temperance lodges were established in most units from the middle of the century. The officer in the centre of this group is the Adjutant, Capt. Bliss.

The Serjeant Major, Staff Serjeants and Serjeants of the 1st Battalion pose alongside the Lucknow Memorial commemorating the heroic defence of the Residency by their forebears in the 32nd Foot. This photograph, taken in 1898, clearly shows the ruins of the Residency in the background.

An informal group of officers of the 1st Battalion at Lucknow in 1898. The vividly striped jackets, were known as 'blazers' (the dark double-breasted garments still worn today are more correctly termed 'boating jackets'). The officer sitting cross-legged is 2nd Lt Herbert Carter who was to win the Victoria Cross five years later.

The Colours of the 1st Battalion at Lucknow in 1898.

Mrs Keveth of St Breward in Cornwall had seven sons, all of whom joined the Army – six in the DCLI. She received the following letter from the Queen's Private Secretary: 'Her Majesty considers the fact of seven sons of one family serving in the Army, all with exemplary characters, reflects infinite credit on themselves and on the parents who have brought them up. The Queen desires that you will congratulate Mrs Keveth, give her £10 and a framed portrait of Her Majesty which I send herewith, and tell her how glad the Queen is to think of this fine example of good and honourable service to their Sovereign and Country from the sons of a single Cornish family!'

The Regimental Depôt in Bodmin was housed in some extremely handsome stone buildings set among well laid-out grounds. This is the officers' mess, in around 1900, when the Depôt had been occupied for twenty years.

Officers of the 2nd Battalion at Raglan Barracks, Devonport, shortly before sailing for South Africa on 4 November 1899.

The same officers after a few weeks active service in South Africa.

Members of the Cyclist Company of the 1st Volunteer Battalion at camp near Helston in around 1900. The 1st Battalion continued to wear its rifle regiment uniforms long after most of the volunteers had changed to infantry of the line scarlet.

Soldiers never change: a group of men from the 2nd Battalion pose outside a field cookhouse in South Africa. Although this view was taken in about 1901, it could at first glance be mistaken for soldiers of any period in the last hundred years. Note the wide variety of dress and equipment. When columns were operating away from the railway lines of communication, rations often consisted of little more than hard tack biscuits – hence the widespread custom of shooting for the pot.

Lord Mount Edgcumbe, Lord-Lieutenant for Cornwall, bidding farewell to the composite draft from the two Volunteer Battalions which was due to sail for South Africa the following day in February 1901.

Members of the 2nd Volunteer Battalion in camp, summer 1902. Many volunteer units adopted this somewhat strange combination of dress, wearing khaki slouch hats (similar to those issued to troops in South Africa) with their scarlet serge tunics.

During the latter part of the South African War (1899-1902), the British erected a network of blockhouses in an attempt to curtail the movement of the Boer Commandos. These blockhouses, which were normally constructed of two skins of corrugated iron filled with stones and earth, were sited so that each was in visual contact with its two neighbours. Any attempted movement through the net could be immediately detected and a mobile reaction force summoned up. Most of the blockhouses lay along railway tracks which ensured a reasonably quick response. This photograph shows one such blockhouse taken from a military train.

A close-up of a typical blockhouse. The garrison, consisting of half a platoon, was commanded by a junior officer or a Serjeant. Life inside must have been almost unbelievably tedious. Sjt William Roberts (the large man shown fourth from the right in the rear rank) commanded this particular blockhouse. He is depicted in a more formal photograph on the next page.

William Roberts, now a Colour Serjeant, photographed with his wife and two children at the Regimental Depôt around 1905.

Parades of great magnificence were held in the most far-flung corners of the Empire to mark Royal occasions quite regardless of whether there was anybody to watch them. This is the 1st Battalion celebrating the Coronation of King Edward VII in Ceylon in 1901. The audience appears to number a total of eleven!

Troops, including a draft for the 2nd Battalion, embarking from the Great Western Railway quay at Devonport ready to be ferried out to their troopship which was to take them out to South Africa in about 1901.

Officers of the 2nd Battalion returning from South Africa in 1903.

While the 2nd Battalion was fighting the war in South Africa, the 1st Battalion was relegated to the somewhat ignominious role of guarding Boer prisoners in Ceylon.

The Cyclist Company of the 1st Volunteer Battalion in camp on Salisbury Plain, August 1903. Note the blanket rolls carried by the men (but not by the two officers who must have spent chilly nights). The Company Commander appears to have been a regular officer as he is wearing a Queen's South African medal with several clasps. His sword is attached to his bicycle frame, which conjures up visions of him leading a gallant charge of cyclists with drawn sword!

A glimpse of the future: a Clement-Talbot motorcar, the eleventh to be registered in Cornwall, stands outside the Depôt Officers' Mess at Bodmin in 1904. The owner, Capt. Stericker, is behind the wheel; the officer to the left is Capt. Norris, the Quartermaster, and the officer to the right is Capt. Burder. Capt. Stericker's charger, Kitty (watched over by a groom), does not seem particularly interested in this strange new form of transport.

Maj. Herbert Carter, DCLI, attached to the Indian Army, was awarded the Victoria Cross for his gallantry in rescuing a Sikh soldier on 19 December 1903. Maj. Herbert Carter died during the First World War during a long forced march to relieve the besieged garrison of Mwele-Mdogo in German East Africa. Maj. Carter came from Exeter in Devon.

Elaborate decorations in the Guildhall, Plymouth, for a ball given by Lt-Col. Morris and the officers of the 2nd Battalion, on 6 April 1904, after their return home from South Africa.

The 1st Battalion Bugles, probably at Wynberg, South Africa in about 1904. Although the 1st Battalion took no part in the fighting during the South Africa War, it was one of the first units to serve in the Army of Occupation following the Boer surrender in 1902.

A shooting team of the 2nd Volunteer Battalion at the Depôt in 1905. The be-medalled soldier in the centre of the rear rank has seen considerable active service with both regular battalions. He is wearing the 1884/85 Egypt medal, the Indian medal with 1897/98 clasps, the 1899 Queen's South African Medal, the Long Service and Good Conduct Medal and the Khedive Star.

Members of the 2nd Volunteer Battalion shooting on Grogley Halt range in 1905. Rifle shooting became an obsession with many volunteers. Matches were eagerly contested and winning teams and individuals were rewarded with very handsome silver cups, shields and medals. Some of the local ranges seem to have been constructed with little regard to safety standards. This particular one was a Grogley Halt, one of several such halts on the Bodmin/Wadebridge railway line which ran down the Camel Valley.

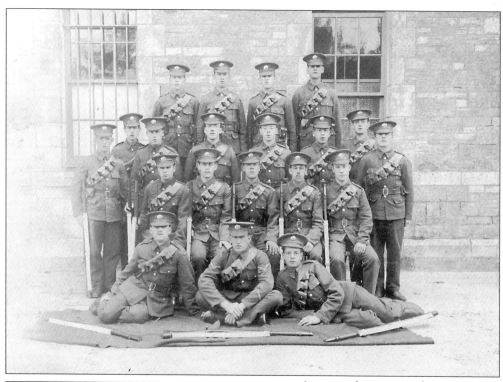

A group of recruits at the Depôt clearly showing the newly introduced bandolier equipment in 1906. The use of this equipment was a short-lived experiment based on the unofficial practise which evolved during the South African War and was aimed at achieving simplicity and the need to cut down the weight carried by the infantry soldier.

Lt Clement Smith, DCLI, attached to the Somali Mounted Infantry. Awarded the Victoria Cross for his gallantry in attempting to rescue a Somali soldier who had been surrounded by hostile tribesmen on 10 January 1904. He later commanded the British/ANZAC Camel Brigade under General Allenby in the Palestine Campaign of 1917. Lt Smith came from the Isle of Wight.

The 2nd Battalion Serjeants' Mess visiting HMS *Cornwall* in Gibraltar dockyard in 1906. HMS *Cornwall*, an armoured cruiser, was to play a prominent part at the Battle of the Falkland Islands eight years later when, although seriously damaged, she sank the German cruiser *Liepzig*.

The 2nd Battalion small bore shooting team, Gilbraltar, 1906. The Broderick forage cap, seen here being worn by the two NCOs was one of the most unpopular items of uniform ever issued to British soldiers. It was withdrawn after only four years.

The 1st Battalion officers' dinner to celebrate the fiftieth anniversary of the Defence of Lucknow held in the mess of Cambridge Barracks, Woolwich, on 13 December 1907. Among the guests was Mr A.M. Inglis, son of General Sir John Inglis, late of the 32nd Foot who had commanded the garrison. Mr Inglis, although only a small boy at the time, had been present throughout the siege. Note the ragged state of the 1st Battalion Colours which had been in service since 1885.

Trials of an early form of mechanical troop transport on Salisbury Plain in 1908. This cannot have been much faster than marching, but at least it relieved the soldier of considerable physical effort and allowed heavier weights of ammunition, rations and stores to be carried.

Officers of the 1st Battalion on the last day of Autumn manoeuvres, September 1909.

A group photograph of the officers of the 1st Battalion taken at Gravesend in 1910. The Commanding Officer (fourth from the left, back row) is Lt-Col. E.S. Burder, while Adjutant (second from the left, front row) is Lt B.E.W. Childs.

The 1st Battalion taking part in the Proclamation of King George V at Gravesend in 1910.

The Coronation of King George V, 1910. The 1st Battalion lining the processional route around Piccadilly Circus. Their dipped Colours can be clearly seen on the left of the photograph.

The Cyclist Company of the 5th Battalion (Territorial Force) on parade outside Webb's Hotel, Liskeard, in 1910. The rifles are .303in Martini Henry carbines, weapons that had been obsolescent for almost twenty years.

The Farriers section of the Cornwall Squadron, Royal 1st Devon Yeomanry, in 1910. The Royal 1st Devon Yeomanry was the senior Yeomanry regiment in the British Army and was thus privileged to wear the unadorned Royal crest (the crown surmounted by a lion) as its cap badge. Although the word 'Cornwall' did not appear in the regimental title, it always had one squadron based in Truro.

The Farrier Serjeant of the Cornwall Squadron, Royal 1st Devon Yeomanry, photographed with one of his smiths in 1910.

The German Emperor, Kaiser Wilhelm II, arriving by special train at Port Victoria, Isle of Grain, on 23 May 1910 to board the Imperial Yacht *Hohenzollern*, having attended the funeral of his uncle, King Edward VII. He is greeted by a Royal Guard of Honour mounted by the 1st Battalion, (commanded by Capt. Robert Olivier) which was stationed at Gravesend. This is one of the very few existing photographs which shows the Kaiser's withered left hand.

The Band and Bugles and Escort to the Colours of the 2nd Battalion about to leave the Depôt to lay up their Colours in St Petroc's parish church, Bodmin, on 26 April 1911.

HRH The Prince of Wales and HRH Prince Albert outside the Depôt Officers' Mess on the 16 March 1911.

The troop train, carrying the 2nd Battalion to Mafeking for the 1911 annual manoeuvres, broke in half during the night without anyone in the front portion being aware of the mishap. Here the train is halted on the veldt at dawn as a relief engine brings up the missing coaches. The officer standing alone on the left of the photograph, in what was remarked as being 'a characteristic attitude', is the Adjutant, Capt. Arthur Stericker.

The 1st Battalion Mounted Infantry Section at Aldershot in 1912. This was an absolutely plum command for an infantry subaltern with tactical imagination and a love of horses. The concept of Mounted Infantry originated from the need for mobility over long distances in the South African War. Mounted Infantry were however never employed in the First World War.

The machine-gun section of the 1st Battalion at Tidworth in 1912. The guns are Maxims which were shortly to be replaced by the Vickers. In spite of the pleas of Lt-Col. N. R. McMahon DSO, The Chief Instructor of the Small Arms School, Hythe, the British Army only had two machine-guns per battalion when it first went into action in 1914, hence the vital need for every rifleman to be able to produce accurate and very rapid fire.

Officers of the 3rd (Reserve) Battalion at Summer camp at Fort Tregantle in August 1913. This must have been almost the last time that the old 'Militia' turned out in its full military splendour.

'B' Company of the 1st Battalion at Tidworth, 1913. In less than a year these men would be involved in one of the epics of British military history at Mons, Le Cateau, the Aisne and Ypres. The fact that this group only shows forty-nine men, when the full establishment of a company was over a hundred all ranks, demonstrates how most 'home' battalions were far below strength in peacetime. On mobilization for war, this shortfall was made up by calling up Reservists.

Three
Armageddon
1914-1918

Britain went to war in 1914 with a small, highly trained volunteer army – minute in size compared to the great conscripted forces of the other European nations. Known to the Kaiser as 'that contemptible little army', 'The Old Contemptibles', as they were proud to call themselves, were initially all we had to put in the field. They fought with the greatest valour against overwhelming odds. In that first year the old British regular infantry was nearly annihilated. At the outbreak of war, Field Marshal Lord Kitchener immediately set about raising a new volunteer army. The response was overwhelming and by the Spring of 1915 the 'New Army' battalions were beginning to cross to France. Not until 1916 was a single British soldier conscripted; before this, Britain fielded the greatest volunteer army in her history. The 1st, 2nd, 1/4th, 1/5th, 6th, 7th, 8th and 10th Battalions of the DCLI fought in various theatres of war, while a further six battalions provided the vital reserve and training capability.

The telegram to the Depôt ordering mobilization, 4 August 1914. The majority were greatly elated, confident that war would be over by Christmas. The 1st Battalion was a 'home' battalion which, in accordance with the policy of the time, was far below war establishment. Accordingly 650 Reservists were posted in to bring the battalions up to a strength of 1,023 all ranks.

The 1st Battalion entraining at the Curragh siding at 7a.m. on 13 August 1914, preparatory to moving to Dublin docks. The Regimental History states: 'The ladies of the Regiment bid the Battalion farewell and displayed typically British fortitude under the circumstances which were most trying'. Within a few weeks many of these ladies would be widows and many of the officers and soldiers depicted in the photograph would be dead.

The 2nd Battalion was stationed in Hong Kong at the outbreak of war. The Royal Navy were immediately given the task of rounding up German merchant shipping in the China Sea and, if possible, sinking the German cruiser *Emden*. Because the Royal Marines on the China Station were well below war establishment, the complement of HMS *Triumph* was augmented by officers and men of the DCLI.

The French cruiser *Duplex* which escorted the 2nd Battalion on the first leg of its journey from Hong Kong to England in 1914. French warships were built to idiosyncratic designs, seldom resembling those from any other nation.

When the 2nd Battalion sailed from Hong Kong for home in the troopship *Nile* on 21 September 1914, it was escorted in the latter part of the journey by the Imperial Russian cruiser *Askold*, an ancient looking warship with five very tall funnels. On arrival in England the officers of the Battalion were entertained by the Russians in what was long to be remembered as an alcoholic marathon. At this party the Regiment presented their hosts with a silver cigarette box while in return they received a traditional Russian silver gilt drinking vessel, called the Askold Cup, decorated with intricate enamel and filigree work.

The 3rd (Reserve) Battalion at Falmouth during the very early days of the First World War. It is interesting that the term 'Great European War' appears to have been coined within a few weeks of the outbreak of hostilities.

Soldiers of the 6th Battalion taken on 18 August 1914 at Watts Common, Aldershot. These men were probably reservists who formed an advance party to organize the tented camp ready for the great influx of recruits on 5 September. The 6th Battalion was the senior Kitchener battalion of the DCLI. From the very start it was an extraordinarily happy and proud unit. The Battalion sailed for France on 7 June 1915 as part of the 14th Infantry Brigade. It took part in some of the heaviest fighting in both the Ypres Salient and the Somme. Known as 'the Shiny Sixth' it quickly earned a name for itself as one of the finest battalions in battle.

Soldiers of the 3rd (Reserve) Battalion in their tented camp at Falmouth, September 1914.

A procedure as familiar to today's infantry soldier as it was to those of the First World War. Foot inspection in the village of Morlancourt where the 1st Battalion was resting in 1914.

A soldier of the 1st Battalion uses a somewhat Heath-Robinson contraption to fire his rifle without exposing himself to the enemy, probably taken near Messines in December 1914.

Soldiers of the 1st Battalion attempt to dry out somewhere behind the front line in the Ypres Salient in December 1914. Rain, mud and hard service have taken their toll on the appearance of these men whose turnout, only four months previously, would have been immaculate.

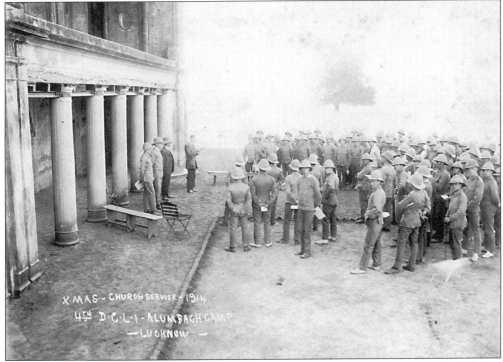

The 1/4th Battalion (Territorial Force) attending a Christmas Day Service at the Allambagh, Lucknow, shortly after their arrival in India in 1914. The Allambagh was of key importance during the siege when the Regiment defended Lucknow in 1857.

The 1st Battalion in the trenches on the Messines Ridge, January 1915. A sketch made on the spot by Pte William Ferguson.

The entrance to the Ypres Cellars in which sixty officers and men of the 6th Battalion were killed while resting on 12 August 1915.

A 1st Battalion trench on the Messines Ridge, January 1915. A battalion report on morale stated: 'The men appear to be resigned to trench warfare and there is very little grumbling at its hardships. In their letters they invariably express a desire to "go over the top", but how genuine their desire is, it is hard to decide. They take practically no interest in drills, etc when back in billets, taking them as a necessary evil connected with rest to be got through with as little effort as possible'.

A trench occupied by the 1st Battalion on the Messines Ridge in January 1915. This was a particularly hard winter. Goatskin jackets were beginning to arrive at the front but were by no means a general issue.

A group of 3rd (Reserve) Battalion soldiers at Falmouth in early 1915. The man sitting second from the right is Charles Burt who was destined to be killed at Ypres on 4 October 1917.

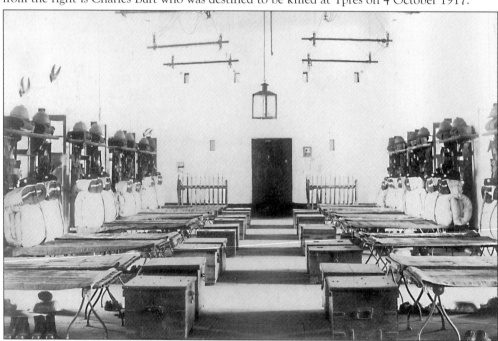

A 1/4th Battalion barrack room at Raniketi, 1915. This sort of accommodation would have been perfectly familiar to soldiers a hundred years previously. Note the bars suspended from the ceiling to which *punkahs* would have been attached in hot weather. *Punkahs* were large swinging cloth covered frames which served as fans. They were kept in motion all night by *punkah wallahs* who sat or lay outside pulling cords which led indoors through holes in the wall and were attached to the *punkah*.

The rigours of trench warfare: anybody who has ever served in the infantry knows the vital importance of constant brews of hot sweet tea which must, on no account, be disrupted by enemy intervention. Tickler's Plum Jam (bottom right) was part of the soldier's staple diet on active service and became the subject of much cynical humour.

L/Cpl Rendle VC appears to be failing to impress a somewhat elderly citizen of Porkellis during the 3rd Battalion recruiting drive in May 1915.

L/Cpl Rendle VC holds up his decoration as he addresses crowds at St Minver during the countywide recruiting drive organized by the 3rd Battalion in May 1915.

Gentlemen of the Press follow the 3rd Battalion recruiting drive. The Regiment's reception at each town and village was reported in great detail, complete with the number of recruits that had come forward. Bodmin had the worst record, while Padstow had the best.

Lt-Col. John Verschoyle had a remarkable career which spanned forty-four years of service. Commissioned into the 46th Foot in 1874, he fought at El Magfar, Tel-el-Mahuta, Kassassin and Tel-el-Kebir – the last actions in which British infantry went into battle wearing scarlet. After commanding the 1st Battalion in South Africa he went on to command a Volunteer Brigade before retiring in 1901. On the outbreak of the First World War he was, like many other elderly officers, temporarily recalled to raise a Kitchener battalion. However, such was his physical toughness, skill at absorbing new military doctrine and popularity with his soldiers (all ranks called him 'Daddy Verschoyle') that he was allowed to remain in command rather than hand over to a younger man. He took his Battalion, the 8th, to France in 1915, and thence to Salonika at the end of that year. Seldom can any officer have seen such radical change in battlefield conditions. His daughter, Hope, remained a most loyal supporter of the Regiment and, almost to the end of her life, would make her way across London to attend Old Comrades Association meetings. She died in 1996 at the age of ninety-three.

The Officers' Messes in India did not lack for staff, even during the First World War. This is the native element of the 1/4th Battalion mess staff at Bareilly in about 1915. The man sixth from the right in the centre row wears the India General Service Medal with two clasps (probably North West Frontier, 1908 and Abor, 1911-12).

Two Territorial soldiers of the 5th Battalion in 1915. Note the 'Imperial Service' badge worn on the right breast of the taller of the two men. This denoted a pre-war declaration that the wearer was prepared to serve outside the United Kingdom on mobilization (the Territorial Force could normally only be deployed within the United Kingdom). Also note the 1914 pattern leather equipment which was widely issued during the first years of the war due to the shortage of 1908 pattern web equipment.

A soldier of the 1st Battalion in the Somme area, Winter 1916.

Mills grenade training with the 3rd (Reserve) Battalion at Freshwater, Isle of Wight, in 1917.

It would seem to have been obligatory for a soldier stationed in Cairo to be photographed on a camel in front of the Sphynx. It must have provided a lucrative trade for the local photographers. This shows NCOs of the 1/4th Battalion in 1917.

The 1st Battalion banner displayed in the Royal Albert Hall on the occasion of a Choral Commemoration of the first seven Division to land in France on 15 December 1917. This banner is now preserved in St Petroc's church, Bodmin.

Cpl William Harmer MM who served with the 10th (Pioneer) Battalion. This study of a First World War soldier is reminiscent of the famous war memorial at Paddington station by C.S. Jagger.

The 10th Battalion repairing a pontoon bridge across the Canal de L'Escaut on 8 October 1918, with the help of German prisoners. Note the partially submerged field gun with its team of dead horses.

DCLI stretcher-bearers carrying wounded back from the front. This photograph was taken by Capt. T.H. Livingstone MD, FRCS of the Royal Army Medical Corps. Note the 18pdr field gun waiting at the roadside; also the signaller up the telegraph pole on the right, presumably repairing lines.

The Signal that informed units that four years of the most bloody fighting in history was to cease at 11a.m. on 11 November 1918. The text reads: From: 20 Div / To: (T) DCLI / Following from 17th Corps timed 0655. / Hostilities will cease 1100 hours today November 11th. / Troops will stand fast in line reached at that hour which will be reported by wire to Corps HQ. Defensive precautions will be maintained. There will be no intercourse of any description with the enemy.

Four
The Lean Years
1918-1939

The First World War was deemed to be the war that was to end all wars. Certainly few people foresaw that in just twenty years Britain would once again be fighting Germany. The nation was near to bankruptcy; many of her finest men were dead; commerce and industry slumped and much of the working population went hungry. It is no wonder that governments could find little money for the armed forces. Between 1919 and 1935 the Defence Budget was reduced in real terms in each successive year. It must have been a frustrating time for a professional soldier. Funds would only cover the most basic forms of training. Drill and ceremonial were however cheap, and it is in these inter-war years that one sees the military mind all too often constricted to the worship of polished equipment and immaculate turnout.

The British Empire still appeared inviolate but, nearer home, the United Kingdom itself was showing ominous signs of fragmentation and in 1922, the thirty counties of Southern Ireland broke away to become a Republic. The 2nd Battalion DCLI was the last British unit to mount guard on Dublin Castle.

They don't make Regimental Serjeant Majors like this today! Walter Bland enlisted in the Grenadier Guards in 1904 and transferred to the Welsh Guards on its formation in 1915, with whom he won the Military Cross as a Company Serjeant Major. In 1919 he transferred to the DCLI as Regimental Serjeant Major of the 1st Battalion in Ireland. There he had the extremely difficult task of rebuilding a post-war regular battalion which was almost immediately thrown into internal security duties in Belfast.

Soldiers of the 2nd Battalion carrying out internal security duties in Dublin 1921.

A GS Wagon of the 2nd Battalion. In spite of the traumatic events taking place in the city of Dublin, a very great pride was taken in the turnout of horses and vehicles.

The 2nd Battalion parade at Wellington Barracks, Dublin, on 31 January 1922 prior to its withdrawal from Ireland. The Battalion had handed over the Dublin Castle Guard to the Irish Army on the previous day, the last British unit ever to perform this duty.

The 2nd Battalion (nearest the camera) in the Square, Cologne, during an inspection of the Brigade by Lord Derby.

The 2nd Battalion produced outstanding cross country running teams every year during the period 1922 to 1929, winning the Rhine Army or Command cup in each of these years and the Army cup five times in succession from 1925 to 1929. No other regiment or corps has ever approached this record.

The Stallards were a family which probably held the record for service in the Regiment. The first recorded Stallard served with the 46th Foot in 1830. This photograph shows Capt. F. Stallard with his four sons, three of whom followed him into the DCLI.

Fraternization at Waan Camp, British Army of the Rhine, 1923. The girl looks well pleased with herself, as well she might, being surrounded by sixteen sturdy young men of the 2nd Battalion

Bandsmen and Buglers of the 2nd Battalion pose in a somewhat inebriated state outside the wet canteen at Longerick Camp, Cologne, in 1923.

Soldiers relaxing in camp near Cologne, 1924. The 2nd Battalion formed part of the British Army of Occupation of the Rhine from 1922 to 1924.

The opening of the Regimental War Memorial in front of the Depôt by the Colonel-in-Chief, HRH The Prince of Wales, in 1924. The bronze statue of a private soldier sculpted by L.S. Merrifield commemorates the 255 officers and 4,027 other ranks who died in the First World War, 1914-18.

The Colonel-in-Chief, HRH The Prince of Wales, talking to Old Comrades and widows at the opening of the Regimental War Memorial on 17 July 1924. The gentleman second from the right is ex-Serjeant H. Cooper who was blinded at Paardeberg where he won the DCM.

A 2nd Battalion barrack room in Malplaquet Barracks, Aldershot, 1928. The iron beds could be telescoped during the day to save space and to provide an improvised easy chair. Note the polished brass plate above each bed which was stamped with the soldier's name and number. Also note the drill rounds on the lower shelf, also highly polished, which were used in weapon training.

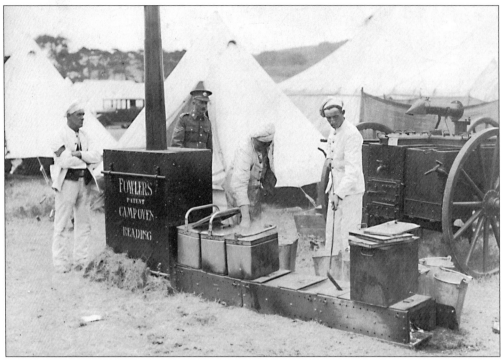

A 2nd Battalion field kitchen in the Aldershot area, 1928.

A 2nd Battalion Platoon competing in the Evelyn Wood Competition at Aldershot in 1928. Platoons had to carry out a forced march of ten miles in two hours immediately followed by a very demanding shoot which included 'run downs' between the firing points from 600 to 100 yards.

The 4/5th Battalion, winners of the Territorial Army machine-gun Cup, 1929. Left to right, back row: L/Cpl Hill, L/Cpl Broom, L/Cpl Williamson, L/Cpl Pentecost. Middle row: L/Cpl Courts, Sjt Walters, Sjt Green, L/Cpl Tann. Front row: Capt. Rushton, RSM Shipp. The team surpassed all its previous records by scoring 92 out of a possible 96 points.

Holders of the Long Service and Good Conduct Medal photographed at the Depôt in 1930. The reversed chevrons worn on the left sleeve by Lance Corporals and Privates denoted various periods of Good Conduct (or undetected crime as it was often called). One chevron for two years, two for five years, three for twelve years, four for sixteen years and five for twenty one years.

The old Colours of the 2nd Battalion about to be trooped for the last time at Aldershot on 9 July 1931.

HRH The Prince of Wales, Colonel in Chief of the Duke of Cornwall's Light Infantry, presenting new Colours to the 2nd Battalion at Aldershot on 9 July 1931. The old Colours had been presented in Bloemfontein on 9 November 1910.

Before 1960 the Royal Cornwall Show was held at various venues around the county. Here the Prince of Wales, Duke of Cornwall, is seen arriving at the showground near St Austell in 1924. The Guard of Honour is mounted by the 4th/5th Battalion (Territorial Army).

A 1st Battalion mule cart at Bareilly in 1931. These light carts provided most of an infantry battalion's transport in India up to 1939. Mules were hardier and more sure-footed than horses.

The Spanish Commandant of Algeceras with his staff during an official visit to HE The Governor of Gibraltar, General Sir Charles Harrington. A Vickers machine-gun detachment of the 2nd Battalion demonstrates its drills outside South Barracks.

The 2nd Battalion King's Birthday Parade, Europa Barracks, Gibraltar, 1932. Europa Barracks square was open to the full force of easterly gales. This was obviously a windy day and the ensign with the Regimental Colour is having great difficulty in controlling it.

The Royal Guard of Honour mounted by the 2nd Battalion in Gibraltar for the Kalifa of Morocco, 1932.

The Ceremony of Keys, Gibraltar, 1933. Sjt C. Edwards and Sjt M. Gallagher of the 2nd Battalion escort the 'Port Serjeant' during the ceremonial locking of the Fortress gates, a spectacle that always attracted large crowds.

The 1st Battalion left Bareilly for Razmak on the North West Frontier of India on 16 October 1934. They travelling north west by train to the broad gauge railhead at Mari Indus, crossing the great River Indus by steamer, and then on a few miles to the narrow gauge railhead at Bannu.

From that point the Battalion took to its feet marching the final 72 miles along a road which climbed to over 7,000ft through some of the wildest, most dramatic country in the world.

Officers of the 1st Battalion at Razmak in 1934. The popular image of soldiering in India being a life of continuous heat and dust is instantly dispelled by photographs such as this one taken on the North West Frontier. The officer in the foreground is Lt-Col. Daril Watson who was to become the Quartermaster General in 1946.

A recruiting drive by the 2nd Battalion in May 1935. Having recently been issued with motor transport, the Battalion took the opportunity to show it off by touring Cornwall with a 'Mobile Column' of thirty-one assorted vehicles. In a time of the severest financial restrictions, the tour was justified as a driver training exercise and a means of running in the new engines. The 'Mobile Column' is seen here at Truro. The commander, Lt John Tilly, speaking to the assembled crowd, said that the infantry now gave an unprecedented opportunity for young men to learn a trade. Three months earlier only two of the sixty members of the 'Mobile Column' had had any knowledge of a motor car.

CSM W. Edwards, 2nd Battalion, winner of the Army Championship King's Medal, the Robert's Cup and the Army Rifle Association Gold Jewel and Bisley, in 1936.

Lt-Col. Carkeet-James commanding the 2nd Battalion at Blackdown with his Adjutant, Lt Tilly in 1936. Carkeet-James had lost an arm during the First World War but had received special authority to remain in the army. He was appointed Governor of the Tower of London in 1945.

The proclamation of His Majesty King Edward VIII at the Shire Hall, Bodmin on 23 January 1936. The Guard of Honour was formed from the Depôt.

Buglers of the 2nd Battalion at the Aldershot Tattoo, 1937.

Brig.-Gen. Martin Turner CB, CMG, CBE. Colonel of the Duke of Cornwall's Light Infantry, 1932-37. Martin Turner led a remarkable life by any standard. Born in 1865 into a middle class family, the eldest of seven children, he enlisted as a private soldier in 1884, only to be promptly traced and bought out by his father. Shortly afterwards however, he again gave his father the slip and, having enlisted in the Gordon Highlanders, was put on a draft to India where he saw considerable active service on the North West Frontier. Commissioned into the DCLI in 1890 he almost immediately found himself involved in more fighting in the Burma War, followed by a period of secondment to the Burma Rifles. In 1912 he fulfilled his ambition by taking command of the 1st Battalion, which he took to France in August 1914. It was largely due to his robust leadership that the Battalion showed such sterling qualities during those first testing weeks. Always up where the fighting was fiercest, he was severely wounded during the crossing of the Marne on 9 September 1914. Martin Turner retired soon after the war, a fighting soldier who, apart from his CB, CMG and CBE was awarded the Order of Danilo, the Order of St Valine and was five times 'Mentioned in Despatches'.

The 2nd Battalion on parade at Malplaquet Barracks, Aldershot, in 1937. Doubtless many of the 'employed' men were not present but even so this photograph shows just how far 'home' battalions had fallen below their establishment. The 2nd Battalion, in the Regimental Journal of that year, reported that, 'shortage of men compelled us to combine our four rifle companies into one training company for individual training'.

The Territorial Battalion carried out a recruiting drive throughout Cornwall in early 1939. This shows the team in Bugle where Sjt Joe Bishop demonstrates the stripping of a Bren light machine-gun. The officer is 2nd Lt Vic Coxen who was later to win a DSO and MC with the Parachute Regiment.

The football team from the German naval training ship *Schleswig Holstein* giving the Nazi salute before the start of a match against the Depôt team at Bodmin in March 1939. The *Schleswig Holstein* was paying a goodwill visit to Falmouth. Five months later she was in action, bombarding the Polish forts which defended Danzig.

The Band and Bugles of the 2nd Battalion at the Tower of London in the Summer of 1939. Their tour of Public Duties brought twenty years of peacetime soldiering to a fitting climax. Two months later the Battalion was on its way to France to undertake very different duties.

Five
The Second World War
1939-1945

The British Expeditionary Force sailed for France in 1939, ill-trained and ill-equipped to confront the air and armour blitzkrieg which Germany was preparing to launch the following year. Military disaster struck in every theatre, and it was not till 1943 that the tide began to turn.

The 2nd Battalion, DCLI, fought in France and Belgium, was evacuated from Dunkirk and, after being re-equipped and re-trained, went back into the fight, first in North Africa and finally in Italy. The 1st Battalion's history was tragic. Thrown into the Battle of the Cauldron near Tobruk on 5 June 1942 against Rommel's armour, and lacking effective weapons, equipment or communications, this proud regular battalion was destroyed in a single day's fighting. The 5th Battalion – a pre-war territorial unit – saw no action till just after D-Day. Landing in France on 22 June 1944, the 5th was, from that day, involved almost continuously in hard fought battles till the German surrender on 5 May 1945.

The Signal to the 2nd Battalion stating that Great Britain was to declare war on Germany at 11a.m. on 3 September 1939.

Prisoners, including members of the 2nd Battalion, being marched back into captivity from Dunkirk, June 1940. Sjt Pittey is nearest the camera with Pte Deakin at his side and Pte Manger behind him. The man wearing a cap is the Battalion's French Army interpreter.

An inspection of DCLI soldiers at the Depôt during the early part of the war. On close examination one can identify at least two distinct types of rifle, indicating the acute shortage of even the most basic of weapons after Dunkirk.

A somewhat motley collection of band and bugle boys at the Depôt in 1940. Boys enlisted at the age of fifteen. Apart from learning their military and musical duties they also continued their schooling under civilian instructors – something denied to most young men from poor backgrounds at that time.

Col. G.E. Wycisk inspects members of the 13th (Bodmin) Battalion Home Guard at Lanivet in 1941. The men are armed with 1914 pattern Canadian Ross rifles – probably the worst service rifle ever produced by any nation. Note the name of the 'Lanivet Inn' is blacked out. All signposts and name boards were either removed or blacked out to confuse enemy invaders. Whether this would have actually worried a German invader is doubtful but it certainly caused considerable confusion to everybody else.

Her Royal Highness The Princess Royal, with Lt-Col. Mercer inspecting ATS at the Depôt, 1941.

Pte Wakefer and Pte Chinner and an unidentified man of the 5th Battalion taken at the 45th Division Battle School in 1942. Note the somewhat unconventional manner of wearing the camp comforter.

Maj. Pengelly leads 'C' Company, 2nd Battalion, towards the front line in Tunisia, March 1943.

Maj.-Gen. Vivian Evelegh, late DCLI, watches his 78th Division going ashore in North Africa in 1942. Admiral Burrough stands to his right.

The German and Italian Armies in Tunisia surrendered at Cape Bon on 13 May 1943. The 2nd Battalion, weary after fighting a succession of particularly tough battles over the previous month, had the satisfaction of seeing their enemies lay down their arms. Here General von Arnim, the German Chief-of-Staff, who was flown to England as a prisoner-of-war, is being received into captivity by Maj.-Gen. Sir Cyril Gepp DSO, late of the Duke of Cornwall's Light Infantry.

The 2nd Battalion vehicles crossing a swollen stream in Italy during the winter of 1944. The present day tourist who visits Italy in the summer seldom realises how cold, wet and bleak this country is in the winter months.

Men of 'B' Company, 2nd Battalion, resting in a railway cutting near Monte Cassino, 13 May 1944. This Company was commanded by Maj. Eldred Banfield. The sleeping figure in the foreground is Sjt Jackson who survived the war. The man to his right is L/Cpl Peachey who was killed three weeks later.

Soldiers of the 2nd Battalion waiting to attack Incontro Monastery, Italy, 8 August 1944.

The Intelligence Officer and the Regimental Serjeant Major, Alfred 'Snowy' Narborough, searching German prisoners after the 2nd Battalion's capture of Incontro Monastery, Italy, on 8 August 1944.

Officers of the 5th Battalion photographed just before D-Day. Within less than a year, nine of these (including the Commanding Officer and Second-in-Command) would be killed and a further eleven wounded.

The 5th Battalion transport halted on a country road in Normandy 1944. Note the prominent white star painted on the door of the 15cwt truck which provided a quick and easy identification between friend and foe. The 43rd Wessex Divisional sign of the Wyvern can just be seen on the front mudguard.

Panther tanks destroyed by the 5th Battalion at Cheux in Normandy, 27 June 1944. This was the Battalion's first action after landing. Sadly the Commanding Officer, Lt-Col. Atherton, was killed.

Another Panther destroyed by the 5th Battalion at Cheux, 27 June 1944.

The original sign erected on Hill 112 near Caen in Normandy. The 5th Battalion held this blood-soaked hilltop for thirteen hours on 10/11 July 1944. Of the 400 men who attacked on the evening of the 10 July, 334 were killed or wounded, including the Commanding Officer, Lt-Col. Dick James.

A Royal Tiger Tank destroyed by the 5th Battalion at Le Plessis, Grimault, in Normandy, July 1944. The Royal Tiger was a very potent machine, being virtually invulnerable to any of the Allied anti-tank weapons. This was the first of its kind ever to be knocked out.

Frank Gillard, the famous BBC war correspondent, interviewing members of the 5th Battalion soon after the end of hostilities in Europe. The officer speaking into the microphone is Capt. B.M. Williams while Sjt 'Ginger' Brice stands between them and the Sniper Serjeant, Sjt John Long. The Regimental Serjeant Major, Reg Philp DCM is on the right of the group.

The telegram announcing the final end of hostilities on 15 August 1945, when Japan surrendered to the Allied power.

The 13th (Bodmin) Battalion Home Guard march past the Mayor of Bodmin, Alderman F. Richards on the occasion of the Victory Parade, 19 August 1945.

Six
Finale
1945-1959

This was the age of the National Servicemen. For the first time the county regiments were recruited almost exclusively from their own counties. Although technically a period of peace, the British Army not only maintained a considerable force in Germany, as part of NATO, but was engaged in a multitude of minor wars and campaigns. Operations in Greece, Palestine, Malaya, Korea, Kenya, Cyprus and Egypt were all carried out by young conscripted National Servicemen. These men accepted their obligations as a fact of life, and undertook their many and often dangerous tasks with skill, courage and an unquenchable sense of humour. Very few National Servicemen would now regret the eighteen months or two years that they spent in the army.

The DCLI saw little active service during this period apart from operations in Palestine, a role that required the very highest standards of self-discipline in the face of extreme provocation. Their tour in the West Indies provided soldiering of a very different and altogether more agreeable nature.

A Universal Carrier of the 2nd Battalion in Greece, 1946. The driver is Pte Bob Lawford. If any vehicle typified the infantry battalion in the war and immediate post-war years it was the Universal Carrier. These tracked, lightly armoured maids of all work were used whenever movement had to be carried out under fire. Apart from being beasts of burden for the machine-gun, mortar, anti-tank and flame-thrower platoons, they were used to re-supply forward troops with ammunition, food and defence stores, and to evacuate wounded. Their armour rendered them impervious to small arms fire and shell splinters, and they had a certain glamour which made them much loved by their crews.

The Colonel of the Regiment, Gen. Sir Walter Venning, receives the scroll on the occasion of the granting of the Freedom of Bodmin to the Regiment on 28 July 1946. The Mayor of Bodmin was Mr Hedley Kinsman, and the town clerk was Mr Ernest Gill.

Her Majesty the Queen Mother accompanied by Lt-Gen. Sir Geoffrey Musson (Colonel of the Regiment) and Lt-Col. John Fry MC (Regimental Secretary) meeting members of the Duke of Cornwall's Light Infantry Old Comrades.

While stationed in Cyprus, in 1947, the 1st Battalion was involved in the detention of Jewish immigrants in an internment camp at Xylotimbu. This task, always unpleasant and often heartrending, arose from the British policy of forbidding Jewish immigration into Palestine. Their ships, bound for Haifa, were intercepted by the Royal Navy and escorted into Famagusta where their human cargoes were unloaded under military guard. Many acts of kindness took place between DCLI soldiers and their charges which are still warmly remembered today.

HM King Paul of Greece visiting the 2nd Battalion at Aliki Camp, Greece, in 1948. Lt-Col. Charles Acland, the Commanding Officer, stands next to the King.

Lt Philip Curtis, DCLI (attached 1st Battalion the Gloucestershire Regiment), was awarded the Victoria Cross posthumously for his magnificent conduct throughout the battle of the Imjin River on the night of 22/23 April 1951. Philip Curtis came from Devonport in Devon.

Green No.1 Dress was first issued to the Band and Bugles in early 1951. Scarlet web belts with white metal lockets were originally worn, but these proved unpopular and were soon replaced with the more traditional white buff. The bugler shown here is Joe Kendall who in later years worked in the Regimental Museum.

The King's Birthday Parade, Salisbury, 1951. The 1st Battalion, under Lt-Col. John Lieching, is seen marching through the city.

119

A silver statuette of a soldier of Fox's Marines presented to HRH Prince Charles, Duke of Cornwall in 1952, to mark the 250th anniversary of the raising of the Regiment.

During the years of the Cold War, a highly complex system existed for the recall of Reservists. This photograph shows a group of none too enthusiastic Reservists reporting for duty with the 1st Battalion at Bordon as part of a mobilization exercise held in 1951.

Two 6pdr anti-tank guns of the 4/5th Territorial Battalion at Summer camp in 1951. Although these weapons were long obsolete in the regular army, they were still issued to Territorials. The towing vehicles are Cambridge Carriers, a slightly larger and more powerful version of the well-tried Universal Carrier.

Capt. John McLaren of the 1st Battalion, (on far left) Master and Huntsman of the Aldershot Beagles in 1951.

'The One and All Club' Korea, 1953. The DCLI reinforcement draft to the 1st Battalion Durham Light Infantry were not split up but served together in the company commanded by another Cornishman, Maj. Johnny Tresawna DSO. Maj. Tresawna, who was later killed, is pictured in the centre of the second row from the front.

A 17pdr anti-tank gun of the 1st Battalion at Minden in 1953. This was the heaviest weapon ever issued to the infantry, and was responsible for much vitriolic language by crews manhandling it into forward positions at night. Nevertheless, the 17pdr was an outstanding gun which, with its immensely high muzzle velocity, was capable of penetrating any tank of that period. The towing vehicle is an Oxford Carrier.

A Vickers machine-gun detachment of the 1st Battalion at Minden in 1953. This is an excellent study of that splendid old workhorse – the Universal Carrier. Note the battalion identification numeral on the right mudguard, and the 6th Armoured Division 'tac sign' on the left.

A posed photograph of a 3inch Mortar detachment of the 1st Battalion taken at Minden in 1953. Soldiers would normally not have worn such immaculate battle dress for training.

When Herr Adenaeur, the Chancellor of Germany, attended the Bermunda Conference of 1954, he was received by a Guard of Honour mounted by the 1st Battalion and commanded by Maj. G.T.G. 'Toots' Williams. This was the first Guard of Honour to be mounted on the island by British troops since 1939.

Soldiers of the 1st Battalion Anti Tank Platoon helping sailors to unload medical supplies over a beach in Haiti following the hurricane in 1955.

The 1st Battalion, the last British unit to serve in British Honduras, bids farewell to HE the Governor, February 1957.

A 1st Battalion signaller operating a Wireless Set No.19 in the Rulle training area of Germany in 1958. Before the days of miniaturized transistors, a signaller needed to possess considerable brawn as well as brains.

A section from 'A' Company of the 1st Battalion practising river crossing in Germany in 1958. The collapsible pattern of assault boat then in use was extremely heavy and, if its canvas sides were torn, could sink with remarkable speed.

A 17pdr anti-tank gun manned by TA soldiers from St Austell on the ranges of Chickerall Camp in 1959. This photograph shows the barrel at the instant of full recoil and gives some idea of the sheer brute force of this very high velocity weapon.

Cadets from Truro Cathedral School Combined Cadet Force at their Annual Inspection in 1959.

The final parade of the 1st Battalion before amalgamation with the Somerset Light Infantry, held at Mercer Barracks, Osnabruck, on 5 October 1959. Lt-Col. David Tyacke leads his Battalion, followed by the Adjutant, Capt. Ian Feild MC, and the Regimental Serjeant Major, Jan Passmore. The Company Commander of the leading Company is Maj. John Tanner.

Soldiers of the 1st Battalion ready to go on parade for the final 'Retreat' ceremony at Osnabruck on 5 October 1959.

The regimental flag of the Duke of Cornwall's Light Infantry is lowered for the last time on the night of 5th October 1959.